Downers Grove Public Library
1050 Curtiss St.
Downers Grove, IL 60515

9\11-15

Published in the United States of America by The Child's World®
PO Box 326 • Chanhassen, MN 55317-0326
800-599-READ • www.childsworld.com

My First Steps to Math™ is a registered trademark of Scholastic, Inc.

Library of Congress Cataloging-in-Publication Data
Moncure, Jane Belk.
My three book / by Jane Belk Moncure.
p. cm. — (My first steps to math)
ISBN 1-59296-658-6 (lib. bdg. : alk. paper)
1. Counting—Juvenile literature. 2. Number concept—Juvenile literature. I. Title.
QA113.M6685 2006
513.2'11—dc22
2005025693

My three Book

by
Jane Belk Moncure

illustrated by
Rusty Fletcher

This is Little three.

She lives in the house of three.

The house of three has three rooms.

Count them.

It has three windows and three hanging baskets.

Every day Little  three leaves the house to go for a walk.

She jumps three jumps. Can you?

One day Little  finds three little pigs but . . .

the three little
pigs are sad.

"We have lost our houses," they say.

"I will help you," says Little three .

Little  finds . . .

a house of straw

for the first pig.

Then she finds . . .

a house of wood  for the second pig,

and

a house of bricks  for the third pig.

How many houses in all?

The three little pigs are so happy

that they dance a jig.

Now Little  finds three bears.

They are sad.

"We have lost our chairs," they say.

So Little  three finds . . .

a little chair . . .

a middle-sized chair  ,

and a BIG chair  .

How many chairs in all?

The three bears are so happy!
One dances, one plays a drum,

and one blows a horn.

Little 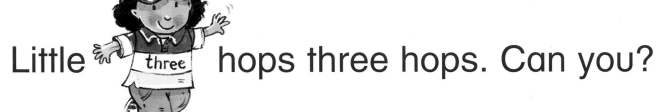 hops three hops. Can you?

She finds one little billy goat, and . . .

then she sees two more billy goats.

How many billy goats does she see?

Away go the three billy goats—

trip, trip, trip—

over the bridge.

Then Little  finds three little mice.

The three mice are sad.
They cannot see very well.

So Little  takes them to the . . .

eye doctor.

She buys them new glasses.
How many pairs does she buy?

The mice are so happy!

The first one stands
on his head.

three

The second
one hops.

The third one
plays a flute.

Little three plays the fiddle . . .

and the three mice dance.
One, two, three. One, two, three.

Little  finds a . . .

three

birthday cake and three candles.

Little  says, "This is my birthday."

She blows out
the candles.

One, two, three.

Little  cuts the cake into . . . .

three pieces.
One, two, three.

She eats two pieces of cake.

Guess what? She leaves one piece of cake for you!

Little  found three of everything.

three pigs

three bears

three billy goats

three mice

three houses

three chairs

three glasses

three pieces of cake

Now you find three things.

Let's add with Little  three .

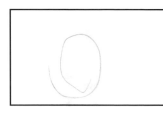   +      =

3   +   0   =   3

   +   =

2   +   1   =   3

Now take away.

3   –   1   =   2

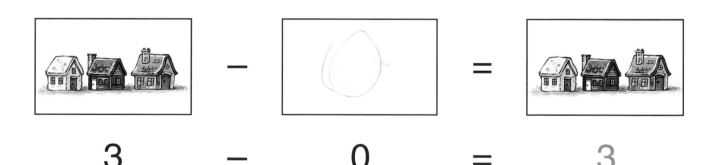

3   –   0   =   3

Little  makes a 3 this way:

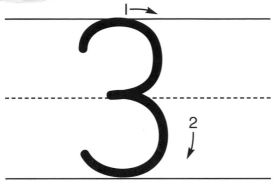

Then she makes the number word like this:

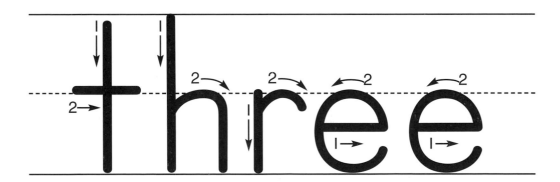

You can make them in the air with your finger.